Mantra Lingua
Global House
303 Ballards Lane
London N12 8NP
www.mantralingua.com

First published in Great Britain in 1997 by Barefoot Books Ltd
First dual language edition published in 2001 by Mantra Lingua
This edition published in 2019

Printed in Letchworth Garden City, UK PE040619PB06198043

پہ ځنګل کې ګرځېدل

Walking through the Jungle

Illustrated by Debbie Harter

Pashto translation by Abu Arabi

پہ جنگل کې ګرځېدل

Walking through the jungle,

ته څه وينې؟

What do you see?

زما په فکر زه یو زمری وینم
چي ما پسي راځي.

د سمندر په سر بنوريدل،

Floating on the ocean,

ته څه وینې؟

What do you see?

I think I see a whale, chasing after me.

Whoosh!

وووهُوش !

زما په فکر زه یو نهنگ وینم
چي ما پسي راځي.

په غرونو کې ختل،

Climbing in the mountains,

ته څه وینې؟

What do you see?

زما په فکر زه يو ليوه وينم
چي ما پسي راځي.

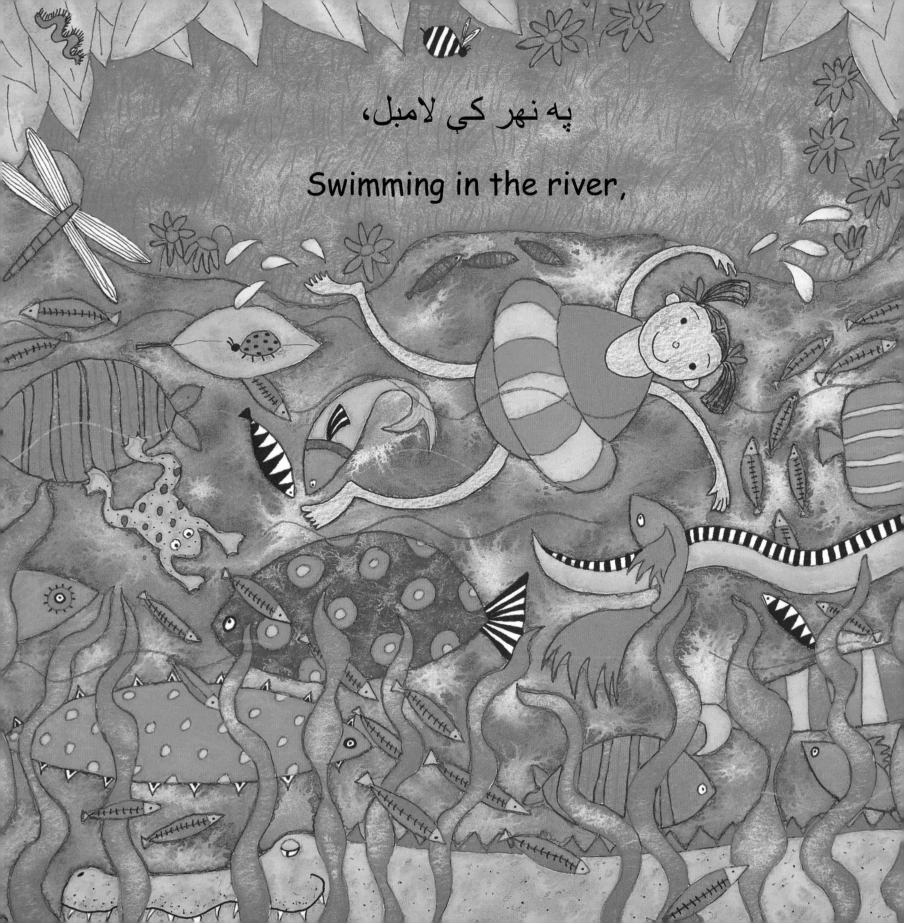

پـه نهـر کـي لامبل،

Swimming in the river,

تە ڤە وینـێ؟

What do you see?

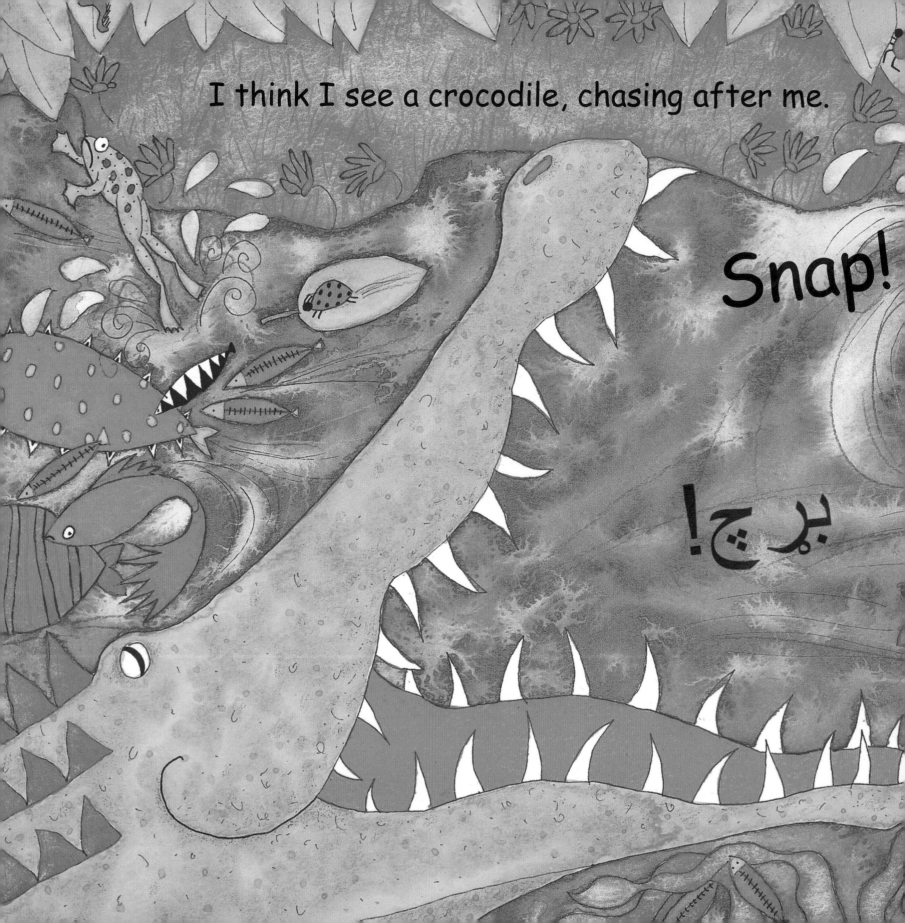

زما په فکر زه یو تمساح وینم
چي ما پسي راځي.

پـه صحرا کې تلل،

Trekking in the desert,